David B. Axelrod

RUSTING

BOOKS BY DAVID B. AXELROD

Poetry

Stills from a Cinema (1968, 1971)
Starting from Paumanok (1972)
Myths, Dreams and Dances (1974)
A Dream of Feet (1976)
*A Meeting with David B. Axelrod
    and Gnazino Russo* (1979)
The Man Who Fell in Love with a Chicken (1980)
Home Remedies: New and Selected Poems (1982)
The End of the Universe (1987)
White Lies (1988)
Resurrections (1989)
A Perpetual Calendar of Poems (1989)
Love in the Keys (1991, 2001)
The Universal Language (1993)
The Chi of Poetry (1995)
Random Beauty (2001)
Another Way (2005)
The Impossibility of Dreams (2007)
Deciduous Poems (2008)
How to Apologize (2009)
The SPEED Way: NASCAR Poems (2012)

Biography

Merlin Stone Remembered (2014)

RUSTING

Ways We Keep Living

Poems by

David B. Axelrod

Taylor & Seale Publishing
Daytona Beach Shores, Florida
2014

For book orders, contact:
Taylor & Seale Publishing
http://www.taylorandseale.com

For readings and workshops, contact:
David B. Axelrod
3WS World Wide Writers Services
1104 Jacaranda Avenue
Daytona Beach, Florida 32118
386-337-4567
axelrodthepoet@yahoo.com

Taylor & Seale Publishing
First Edition
ISBN: 978-1-940224-42-8
LCN: 2014939467

Page and cover layout by WhiteRabbitGraphix.com

Dedication

For my wife, Sandy, and my children,
Jessica, Emily, Daniel and Aileen,
with love and admiration.

ACKNOWLEDGMENTS

Thanks to Mary Custureri and the staff of Taylor & Seale Publishing for their support in bringing forth this book. Thanks to Daniel and Emily Axelrod, Adam Fisher and Lenny Schneir for their assistance and encouragement. Thanks to these editors and publications: "The Impending Election," *The Un-Occupy Movement* (All Books, 2012); "Gallows Humor," "Love Shows," *Rhyme and Punishment*; "Double Books," "Blind, Deaf and Dumb," Walt's Corner, *The Long Islander;* "Rusting," "Old Man Fishing," *North Sea Poetry Anthology: 2009;* "Old Man Fishing," "Solstice," *Long Island Quarterly;* "The Live Oak," featured poem, *Halifax Art League Words and Images Festival;* "Out to Sea," "How to Win Friends," *Poems for the Ages* (Future Cycle Press, 2010); "Declaration of Victory," *13th Annual Performance Poetry Association Literary Review;* "After I Caught My Girlfriend," *Love and Other Passions: Anthology of Central Florida Poets* (CHB Media, 2012); "Two from County Kildare," featured/ published at Gerard Manley Hopkins Festival (2009); "Clorox Clean," *Xanadu Magazine;* "The Snowbird's Lament," "Robot Courtesies," "I Wish I Were," *"How to Win Friends,"* *The Hidden Zone;* "The Snowbird's Sonnet," *A Calendar of Florida Poets, 2013;* "I Want to Love Your Wife," *Merlin Stone Remembered* (Llewellyn Worldwide, 2014); "Fragments of a Sailor's Dream," "Longing," "Misjudgments," *First Literary Review-East;* "ICU Waiting Room," set to music by Pat King and performed by the Long Island Composers' Alliance, Lefrak Concert Hall, Queens College (April 7, 2014); "The Buddhist Bird," *Eternal Snow: An Anthology of Poems;* "Screwing Up," "To Be Somewhere," *Cyclamens and Swords;* "The Horrible Mind," *The Muse — An International Journal of Poetry.*

CONTENTS

THE BUDDHIST BIRD

PREFACE

The muse has been my faithful companion for most of my life. I believe that writing is an important act, and I have found writing — particularly poetry — is a path to wellness. Although the dark content of much of my work may seem to say otherwise, I am happy with my life.

I believe that if I can assist others to a greater appreciation of poetry they, too, will be happier. I measure my own success by two simple criteria. A poem is good for me — both literally and literarily — if it communicates something of importance. By that I mean that a poem should engage our emotions, or at least let us see things in a new light.

Turning my personal toils and troubles, observations and musings into poems must transcend the trivial and confessional. If others read the poems and see something of themselves, that is good. If they learn something new about themselves and others, that is better. If readers and listeners find the poems are a new way of seeing the world, that is the highest measure of success.

I give you these poems as life lessons. I am not just writing poems, I am fostering empathy. Let us share what we have, for better or worse, and make something good of it. I may not be a life coach but I do wish us all a happier existence and these poems are the closest I can come to a survival guide.

— Dr. David B. Axelrod

RUSTING

Self-portrait by David B. Axelrod

RUSTING

Rust populates
those parts of things
that are not touched.

Others are oiled by
fingertips or polished
by the brush of cloth.

Deeper crevices decay.
Even the thickest
iron will grow porous.

For ships, there is
comfort in dry dock,
welders' arcs of light.

For me, just waiting
and wasting. Unlike
love, entropy is slow.

THE HORRIBLE MIND

*Frank Zappa asked "What is the ugliest part
of your body?"*

His first thoughts were often unmentionable —
knives to pare away the pain,
forks to extract apologies.
On second thought, he was aware he
saw things through a specific lens that dis-
torted the world, rendering it a war zone
where Geneva Conventions were ignored —
a torturous place beyond victory
or revenge. "Why do I always hurt
the ones I love?" he asked,
and he could answer without thinking,
"The enemy is hardwired into me."
Some people play computer games
committing endless software murders.
He felt he was under attack. On better
days his mind played word games
called poems, or he resorted to gallows
humor. But the mind loves dirty tricks,
as anyone hiding in his bedroom
could attest — night terrors.

GOTHIC

"The mass of men lead lives of quiet desperation."
— *Henry David Thoreau*

Who needs the clanking
chains, the squeaking stairs
and inexorable footsteps?
There's a cancer ward
in every hospital where
the excisions are torture.

Who needs the bony hand
reaching from the curtain;
the gaunt and bloodless face?
There's a nursing home around
the corner where those who
remember sit waiting for death.

No need to dress in black,
dark makeup, black lipstick,
affectations. There's a girl
in her bedroom cutting herself,
contemplating her own end
before she turns seventeen.

Hollywood works too hard,
rubber masks, 3-D effects,
blood squirting everywhere.
Turn on the lights and film
your neighbors. Face
the camera, film yourself.

WHY SOME PEOPLE DON'T GO
TO HORROR MOVIES.

The abused don't need
Fritz Lang or Alfred Hitchcock.
The images replay like TiVo:
freeze frame, slow motion.
They don't have to build
dark scenery. It's etched
in their mind. There is no exit,
front and rear, in their theater.
Imagine waking in your
own bedroom so lost
you can't find a light that
you wouldn't dare turn on
lest you realize it isn't
a dream. You are there
and it is happening.

LA VIE NOIR

Before we married,
my first wife and I,
walking a moonlit
street in Baltimore,
simultaneously turned
to each other and said,
"Those row houses look
like coffins." We knew we
were in love. The marriage
of two nihilists is dark enough.
Add fits of depression
and you have the perfect
formula for "Noir," cynically
sexual, dangerous if not
criminal, though I always said
if we owned a gun, one of us
would be dead. Instead, we
spawned three talented kids —
each a paradoxical light
in our dark philosophy.
Later, Hollywood taught us
how to make horror movies.

FAITH AND PREJUDICE

Faith begins where reason leaves off.
Someone's child is shot dead by an
angry man. "God has taken that child
to do his work in heaven," a mother says.

Prejudice substitutes for reason.
All so-and-sos are criminals or lazy.
He was wearing a hoodie and looked
suspicious. I stood my ground.

Faith and prejudice go hand in hand.
Because you do not worship my God,
you are not worthy. Kill the infidel.
Drive out the non-believers.

Faith is the prettier name for prejudice.
I do this in God's name. I do this in
the name of your security. Surrender
your human rights to me.

Nothing can prove that your
religion is the one true faith.
God is great. God is good.
God lives in my neighborhood.

If it is built on a lie, it cannot
by its nature, ever be true.

A REASON FOR EVERYTHING

It isn't my business what you
believe or if you stand to pray
or kneel and stick your tongue
out. It's fine that you donate
goats to save Africa, even as you
pay a fortune to buy your stupid
dog his pills or board him in
a kennel. It matters not a fig
who wins our arguments. But
when you tell me, "There is
a reason for everything,"
I worry I could hate you. Sooner,
say you worship Satan because,
then, all the Jews who died,
died for a reason. All people
crushed in earthquakes, children
starving with swollen bellies —
suffer for a reason. All the abuse,
beatings, rapes and wars —
for a reason. What, woman,
could possibly possess you
to believe in such a thing?
It's not for me to forgive you.
I can't forgive myself so
don't ask me. And if there is
some God who planned all this,
I hope you meet Him. Those
who believe in "a reason," deserve
to suffer eternity in such a heaven.

BLIND, DEAF AND DUMB

Romantic love
lays siege to reason

     Love is blind.
     Do tell?

making summer
of any season.

     Must we be deaf
     and dumb as well?

SCREWING UP

Lovers screw up
thinking that love
will conquer all.
They think that
love can change
old habits — the cap
will magically
screw back on
the toothpaste
because, "He loves
to please me."
Instead, the cap
stays off and screwing
up, beyond metaphor,
grows tedious. Couples
drift apart and, with that,
screw around.

AFTER I CAUGHT MY GIRLFRIEND

After I caught my girlfriend
in bed with another man —
worse, a fellow writer whose
talent made me jealous —
I took to my car and drove
two hundred miles in no
direction. The engine did
not overheat or fume. Only
I emitted odorous epitaphs
and curses no catalytic
converter could capture.
Jilted lovers learn to burn
their sorrows into raptures.

WEDDING VOWS

Some see marriage as
a sweet confection but
an honest love does not
conform to rules, absent
of "My way," offering
"Whatever you like." No
obfuscation, no competition.

No gentle greeting
card in my needing you.
Ours is a sacrifice, trading
liberty for imagined pleasures.
You will dress me as
your devoted husband.
I will have my private way.

We will merge our small
finances, make room in
our house for each other's
tastes, all for comfort
through abhorrent aging,
to dance one last dream
act and be complete.

READING OLD LOVE POEMS

"When two divorced people marry,
four people get into bed." — Jewish Proverb

Koheleth said there's nothing
new, but under a brilliant sun
with my lover, even warmth
is reinvented. Then, I think of
poems for my first love, written
that first summer. The body
memory so real — a gritty blanket
on a private strand; we two,
rolling in joy. That was fifty
years ago and now I'm here
with you. Why, much as I love
you, do I still remember her?

FOR THE OLD FLAME I LOCATED ONLINE

In the group shot taken on a lawn
at a summer conference, your smile
is framed by thick red hair. We squint
into the sun — just kids, though we
thought twenty was grown up. We were
instant boyfriend and girlfriend, away
from home and ready for adventure.
The romance lasted a few months,
commuting between two states,
and your reticence to entangle.
All these years I've kept that picture,
following your career — publishing
children's books, a media professional.
I wondered why you never
published a photo I could see —
no public image. I didn't harbor any
fantasy, just curiosity — what became
of you? Until a search told your story:
chronic systemic lupus, from as far back
as when your children were young.
Now, any thought of you as an aging
beauty shining at me if we met
transforms to my sympathy
imagining how you have suffered
and how I dodged a bullet.
If our romance persisted, if we had
married — professionals, city-dwellers,
a cultured family — we would have
spent more time in doctors' offices
than salons and symphonies.

KEEPING AN OPEN MIND

1.
A circular bone saw
buzzes a door
to the brain.
The scalp
bleeds profusely.
How they peel it
back is a surgeon's
job. Within, there's
the gray matter of
changing one's mind.

2.
The brain surgeon
operates, and I'm
awake to report what
neurons do. He removes
my bad habits, replacing them
with more loving ways.
A plate is placed and glued,
the scalp sewn back. After
the gauze unwraps, after
the hair grows long enough
to cover the seamy scars,
no one will know but me.

LONGING

Some things go on too long:
the dentist for more than
a minute; the homily when
you are hungry; the lecturer
who never wears a watch.
Some things could last longer:
our biweekly pay when we
buy groceries and gas;
the cello concert by Yo-Yo
Ma; your caress of my hand
as I pass. Some things should
never stop — this sunshine on
the moist curve of your back.

SOLSTICE

That day breaks should warn us
life is a struggle, wind aimed
over the Atlantic, waves heaving
toward shore. Sun struggles
a shorter day toward winter
while we watch branches bare
their limbs for battle. What
will not bend will break, so frozen
people make the same mistakes:
a daughter of abuse, an alcoholic
husband. Demeter wanting
warmth, asks her daughter, "Why?"

Sunset is a gentle and welcome
state, colors welling in streaks
of cloud, flat strands of sand
at ebb tide. Night rejoices
that it is stronger. We creep
inside, an end to toil, comforted
that darkness lasts much longer.
We need not mourn the death
of flowers: let the tulips have
their rest; wrap tender trunks
to save them; accept what will
not last. Even the sun must die.

APRIL FOOLS

We wait for April, rebirth
programmed into us as surely as
trees are skeletons until sunlight
sets them free from their
dark closets and we, reassured by
a first warm day, open a closet
to put our heavy coat away.

The green of St. Patrick's Day is
inflated to importance by myths
and beer. Spring in northern
climates can be insincere — long
nights and snow that lingers near.
Only when we turn our clocks ahead,
can we see hope for warmer sunsets.

Those who worship Christ,
forgetting he was born in spring,
resurrect him. In April, even poets
begin to sing. Animals unfold
in new-green pastures. Children
come visiting parents who are
glad to pay for trips and tickets.

And the ill, their cancer, for
the moment quelled, postpone
surrender. Facing winter, deaths
climb — January, particularly fatal.
For whatever cold we must endure,
death rates drop in spring.

... and Influence People was a book
my mother always recommended,
but her philosophy was inconsistent,
perhaps because she'd lived through
a depression and the Holocaust. "You're
lucky if you don't give a damn," she'd also
say, "Look at your brother. He'll do
just fine." And who is to say he hasn't
though I can't stand anything about him —
his racist, Rush Limbaugh point of view,
flash temper, homophobic, but somewhat
useful life. He works hard, pays taxes,
has helped raise his wife's family. He's
never so much as collected unemployment.
A successful bastard. Then, there's my
own kid. The youngest, knowing it
offended me, just got a tattoo. Between
whining about money and spending
ceaselessly, you'd think she'd be
respectful of my wishes, but no,
within hours of eighteen it was off
with friends to disfigure her body.
She'll do fine. Not caring about
others' love and feelings should be
the key — much better than a break-
down over some bastard who
ditched you just before your prom.
As for me, I just need to not care,
not treat everyone to dinners, not
squander a hundred hours volun-

teering to help this one's career
and that one's health or heart. Then,
maybe I wouldn't awake with the birds
on a sweaty summer morning wondering
why life is so damned hard and I don't see
the point of loving, or trying, or caring.

MY MOTHER'S PROPHECY

"There's nothing we can do,"
my mother would say, and it
angered me. An abdication
of what parents should be.
Leaving me undefended before
the vehemence of anti-Semites.
"There's nothing we can do."
The only answer for my older
brother's temper even as our
mother loved and cared for
both of us. But what about
the attacks he frequently unleashed
on me? "Nothing we can do."
The answer for all things political
or simply screwed up to the painful
point of surrender. I strove
to prove her wrong — studied,
wrote, created a public face
to prove myself. Until now,
her words soothe me —
a "nothing" that trumps
all other fates. My strivings
diminish. My vanity, though
it persists, is humorous — leaving
"nothing" to console me,
"nothing" to assuage me
and relieve my guilt.

BURNING

1.
It was the morphine they gave her
that focused my mother on the ceiling
tiles in parallel above her bed. "When
those lines meet, they are going to burn
me," she insisted. "Don't let them
burn me before I'm dead." After
the holocaust, my mother didn't believe
in God. She had no place for heaven,
though she did think earth was hell.
After she died we committed her,
lovingly, to the fire.

2.
"That was then. This is now,"
only works if you're superhuman.
Some memories are seared so deeply,
every synapse directs us back to the abuse.
Try rituals, writing the bad thoughts on
slips of paper tossed into a fire, smudging,
incense, exorcism. Nothing short of
immolation can end the pain. Still,
on a May 1st, at some Feast of Beltane,
or perhaps just at a beach bonfire,
it may be possible to purge the past
and bask, instead, in the warmth
of present friendship.

YOUR NATURE

Choose me or not, but the rose
should not resist the bee.
Take me to your center.
There's honey in it, but
first I must have my way.
I don't feel guilty and I
will not sting. Though
such probing can seem
painful — let me tickle.

Or do you prefer to be
my keeper? Restrain me,
spread me to find how,
deep inside, I thrive.
There's no harm in
owning me, your faithful
servant — pollen gatherer,
wax maker, protector
of my queen. Or,

sting me your once
and fatal sting. You
will survive. It is I who
will be sacrificed to
your stubborn nature.

THE SAVIOR

You ask me, "If the house
were burning, what would
you save?" Would it be
my photo albums? Odd how
taking pictures has all but
stopped. I don't own jewelry,
though I imagine gold melting
to nuggets in someone else's fire.
The cat can save itself with
a leap when the door is opened.
I'd see to that, and my wife
is similarly fleet of foot. Yes,
I'd shoo them out. Important
papers? I'd want my kids to
have my will — odd word,
with many meanings, first
asking what we want to do
with life, then how to dispose
of it. My safe, I'm told, is
fireproof to fifteen hundred
farenheit, which will cremate
me, should I linger to breathe
in smoke and choke. Lately,
I wonder if I'd save myself?

SAYING GOODBYE

Saying goodbye to friends
feels easy. It's missing them
that's hard. A colleague
who moved away blogged
for two years — merciless
in his confessions, "I don't know
a soul here. I'm miserable.
I'm lonely." Then, of course,
we mostly stopped hearing.
I've seen him once since,
living with a woman he met
who's driving him crazy.

Family is another story,
good at guilting. "You are
abandoning us. You won't
even see your grandkids."
They'll find a time once
a year to travel down —
but only if I buy their tickets.
Some advise connecting
to them online but that's
like loving a limb that's gone —
phantom sensations. Ether
is a substantial filter.

What interests me is that
simple word, "Goodby." I
always have to type it, then
pause to add the "e" which

seems to me a spelling an-
achronism. But etymologically,
it means, "God be with you."
I'm not even a believer, which
leaves me looking for foreign
alternatives: *ciao, arrivederci,
do svidaniya, zài jiàn, zbogom.*
"Shalom" could work. I settle
for, "See you later."

ON BEING SAFE

His mantra starts out,
"Warm, clean, comfortable."
He's had his share of troubles —
health, work, relationships.
He's never been consoled to hear,
"Others have it so much worse."
Why would that make him feel
better? How many people go hungry,
combing dumpsters for food,
or sleep in cardboard boxes
in freezing weather? Others
may see him as a "kook." At least
he's not a criminal, eying what
others have, ready to pounce.
Nor is he filled with ethnic hatred.
In the darkness of his bedroom,
a cover pulled over his ear,
for a moment, he's grateful he is
not in danger and he can
safely fall asleep.

THE ART OF CAPTIVITY

1.
Who has kidnapped me,
captive, naked every night,
waiting for the beating,
and why does this excite
me? I sweat, pulse racing,
aware I will be forced
and forced again to profess
my love. From this comes
my art, always tightening
around me, even as I
am frighteningly glad.

2.
Those who cast a bronze
know the lost wax must
go somewhere — a vapor
that gives way to form.
When the heat of creation
replaces me — when I give
way to some new shape
awaiting paring and polish —
will anyone remember
that which was me or
all my years of sculpting?

BETRAYAL IS BETTER SERVED

Cold. I know you are thinking, "revenge,"
or perhaps you believe that a good twist
of a knife deep into the back produces
a searing pain. Not so. Those who make
friends lightly break the trust like thin
ice cracking suddenly beneath one's feet.
Imagine the illusion of solidity, the silly
confidence that one can walk on water,
though winter should be a hint not to
trust. Skate out, do a figure eight, smile
until the sudden crack and quicker fall
beneath the ice. That's betrayal for you.
Just when you think you can trust a fellow,
all that you know lets go. You're left
wondering if there are really air bubbles
trapped under the surface or if you'll die
of the brutal cold before you drown.

WAITING TO BE ANXIOUS

Those who are prone are
always waiting, but I'm not.
Two things in my favor —
I'm not an addictive person-
ality and I don't get anxious,
though lately I've thought
I ought to be. So many bridges
burning — retirement,
a house sold, a major
move. Now would be
a good time to feel
that tightness in
the chest, shortness
of breath, flush across
the face and oh, that
ceaseless pulsing. Not
remembering minor facts —
names of old neighbors, places,
dates not even Google can
recover — can keep me up
at night, somewhere between
frustration and fear of Alzheimer's.
Tonight, I'm just awake
with me — mildly curious
to see if I will live through it.

OUT TO SEA

There is a monument by
the sea, commemorating
TWA Flight 800, shot
down off Long Island's coast,
two hundred thirty people
lost. None I know chose
to die, so my walking past it
to commit suicide seems
like a sacrilege. A March
wind pummels me with sand
and salt. I descend eroded
dunes, trek far enough,
past walkers yearning
for spring, to an empty patch.

I once made the perfect plan:
> *Buy a big accidental death*
> *policy; wait months. Then,*
> *at some remote location, dial*
> *911, "Someone is in the surf.*
> *Come quickly." Put the cell*
> *phone, car keys in your shoes.*
> *Swim out and just let go.*

My body would be found
fairly soon. My children
would be left rich. I might
even appear to have died
a hero. I never bought that
policy. Pity, but I have stowed
my ID in the car, taken off

my shoes, placed my keys.
The incidence of waves is
frequent but not violent,
wearing broken shells into
tourist amulets. Gulls have
spotted herring a hundred yards
out and circle wildly. The beach
is littered with brittle bits.

The water is cold enough
to turn my ankles blue.
There's a break in the dunes
that could shelter me, where
I retreat to lie on the softest,
wind-scattered sand. After
an hour spent between
reminiscence and regret,
I stir, put on my shoes,
and, keys in hand, hurting
as if I'd been beaten by
a two-by-four, I trudge
past the monument where,
soon, the flags of thirteen
countries will cling to poles
for those who perished. I return
to the car where a simple
note explains my demise.

I've saved it as a draft —
not badly written.

CLOROX CLEAN

The most effective mix is
ten to one to kill whatever germs.
Overdosing, I pour it straight from
the bottle to the floor. I don't wear
clothes I value. Alone, I might
wear only underwear, spreading
the liquid with a rag as my eyes
tear. I've burned off my fingerprints,
bleached my knees and soles.
Lungs scorched, I cough as I
cry for all my blemishes.

MISJUDGMENTS

The bird, hovering a moment,
slowing, misses its branch.
The squirrel who leaps from
its high perch, crash lands.
The raccoon miscalculates the car.
This is my natural state,
falling, crashing, crushed.
Yet, simply human, I lack
the dumbness of other animals,
with not so much as a mask
to cover my eyes.

BIRD UNDERSTANDINGS

Birds know how to die, anonymously,
only occasionally violating their code,
found mauled by the neighbor's
cat or crusted with gravel along
a road. We nearly never see them
perish, find no trace, though
thousands flock. They do not
trouble us for a funeral.

Imagine bird bone fields
where slight, white skeletons
bleach in beds of feathers,
a thousand wishbones awaiting
our hopeful tug. Or do they simply
fly so high they disappear?
Birds know death doesn't matter.

I WISH I WERE

I wish I were smart.
A smart man can even out-
wit a cheetah who, itself,
runs seventy miles per hour,
its haunches huge springs
releasing energy. I plod along
making my catty comments.
Chimps do somersaults.
I'm often told I'm flippant.
There are those who can
remember vast texts, reciting
them at will. I'm more like elephants —
who truly don't remember much —
perhaps a few commands,
not even old injuries. Well,
I do remember all those
injuries — by my brother, best
friends, even an ex-wife. But
all that just clouds my judgment
and I keep running after brilliant
people, admiring them, asking
if I can be a friend. Why do I
mistake intelligence for moral
fiber? A Ph.D. doesn't guarantee
a bit more kindness. So many
geniuses act monstrously. I'm
left grateful. I'm just smart enough
to love you and dumb enough
to trust you'll kill me quickly if
I've misjudged.

RECRIMINATIONS

Rape victims may blame themselves,
as if just walking home at night invites
attack. But those who were abused,
the earlier in life and longer, are
wired differently. Lying on some
couch for therapy can't keep away
night terrors. There was the boy,
brutalized from birth until his older
brother left, who wondered why
young children, smiling as they passed,
were happy? Those little pokes that
siblings give each other? He knew
only a fist between his shoulders
that knocked him down, breath-
less. Victims may yearn to dup-
licate their agonies, but there's no
excuse for cruelty. If the machine
is that badly broken, junk it.
But how many fathers, brothers,
priests or trusted friends walk free
while their victims suffer silently,
jealous of the joy they never had?

SOME PEOPLE THINK I'M DANGEROUS

Allow me to be dangerous,
my front tooth chipped, my
left molar missing. Maybe
the mercury in my fillings
is dangerous. My hearing,
dim, I'm hardly a proper
snooper. Maybe I'd listen
in on you, but, "Huh? What?
Could you repeat that?"

I was only, briefly, good
at wrestling. My last couple
rounds with gloves on made
me throw up. I don't know
karate, don't own a gun.
Dangerous? I've shrunk
two inches in height since
my first license. It's been
ten years since I could
press two hundred pounds.

If they think I'm a danger
I'll take that as a compliment.
All I have are my words
and they, mumbling fools,
are scared to death of me.

A THING OR TWO

I'll tell you a thing or two about happiness
which, if it is a warm puppy, should be
cooked and eaten. There are absolutely no
absolutes, the consequence of which may
make the religious queasy but will certainly
save on C-4 and martyrs. There may be
a season for everything, but the rich can
go south for the winter. As for book learning,
most textbooks are wrong. The classics are
over-rated. Looking too closely is myopic.
Buddha's middle way, Jesus' turned cheek,
the wisdom of so many other sages, is lost
in the translation — of time, of place, of
tongues tied with bad intentions. Between
the first and last tick, some folks think they
have figured it out and thus smile broadly.
If you cry all the time, they will take you
away, but if you laugh all the time, you're
an f-ing nut case. Get out of your aphoristic,
self-styled head and live. In a hundred years
nearly every one of seven billion souls alive
now will be dead. No matter. Happiness is
an illusion, not even worth the price
of a movie ticket. The reviews are in.
The critics are all thumbs up. It's a life,
whatever that is, and millions more are
lining up, scratching at the door to take
your place. You might as well be happy.

THE BUDDHIST BIRD

Photo by David B. Axelrod

THE BUDDHIST BIRD

From its unseen perch it
calls to me, "Right here.
Right here." It's voice
is clear, it's message
in the moment.

Bayberries are daily
strewn across my
concrete walk. They are
the elderly surrendering
to spring blossoms.

There it is, a cardinal,
red plumage as urgent
as its call, "Right,
right, right here."
We eye each other.

Today, the hickory tree
has resurrected, draping
new leaves, just shy
of flowers. A neighbor
told me it was dead.

I'm not one for bird calls,
but I do my best to answer,
"Now, now, right now."
Cloudy-bright, moist
air. Exquisite.

THE SAILOR'S DREAMS

1.
We could breathe underwater
swimming ever deeper
in a sunlit, emerald sea

unencumbered, naked
skimming hands over wriggling
bodies, kicking feet

until the water darkened
with the depth and we grew
quiet as we floated

slowly upward, hugging
tightly, eyes closed
until we surfaced

to a giggling salty kiss
that signaled our time to dive
still deeper in our love.

2.
The sea speaks patient sibilants
to a softly rushing breeze.
Sometimes a whoosh of a larger
wave warns a wading man.
The sea is an ancient grandma
shushing a rowdy child.

Sit silently to listen —

a distant car, an ice cream
vendor's song, the squawk
of heron gulls dispensed
a snack by a giddy girl.

All sounds are subsumed
by a lesson taught us by
the sea — hush hush
your thoughts. Shh shh
your aspirations. Breathe
softly the salt air.

3.
The air divides with our slow
movement through the room.
I follow in your steps, liquefied
by anticipation. Each article
of our clothing slides up
or down and off, a matching
advance of energy — a dance
of electricity between us.
We turn to hug, joy in our
eyes. I've seen how swallows

slip air currents to soar
curves across the skies.
So I rise toward your
warm sighs, moist currents,
slipstreams for me to ride.

4.
Be my north and I will
be your compass, finding
you steadfastly. Be my
south and I will bend
to your warm breezes.
The west of you makes
me wild. Your east
remains inscrutable.
Encircle me. Be my
world, and I will
delight in exploration.

COMMANDER OF CRABS

At the mouth of the Tomoka
River, a thousand fiddler
crabs line the shell-strewn
shore. I approach slowly,
herding them in columns
to battle each other
in the marshland. They
bob their light purple
shells, menace one large
white claw. Except for
my firm footsteps they
would do only a slightly
sideways shuffle. But I
am their Caesar —
rallying my legions
to die in defense
of their land.

COMING TO REST

1.
A southwest wind sweeps
through the saw palmetto.
The surf massages
a thin stretch of sand.
Pelicans have spotted
a school of whitebait.
The sploosh of their
headlong dives reminds
me of my appointed rounds.
I'd start the car but wait —
the breeze has begun
to stroke the whiskers
of a single sabal palm.

2.
The forest that blurred
at interstate speed now
beckons at the rest stop.
Push through the dusty
underbrush. Disappear
into pines. Observe
lichen-covered stones
strewn amid hackberry
and loblolly. Breathe
deeply of turpentine
air. Sink slightly into
years of pine straw.
Allow yourself to root.

GUILTY

A salt mist rises along the shore.
A steady wind renders sunrise
cool to the skin despite the warmth
of summer. Who first noticed
the horizon curves or mused that
the sun does not sizzle rising
from the sea? We live in this
fortunate land where others lived
long before us. As far down
the beach as we can see, were
tribes we met and murdered,
then scraped from the curve
of memory. Oceans matter,
lasting longer than aristocracy.
Salt pounds to vapor, rising in
the swells that break on the beach.
What we have now was stolen.
Shouldn't we, witness to such
beauty, feel guilty?

NO BIG DEAL

Reading the *New York Times*
over a plate of leftover rice and meat
for brunch, I try not to cry. Somewhere
between oil-soaked pelicans and Uzbek
children bleeding, I want to be inured.
If I cry, let it be for little things like
illness and mortality. The daily cruelty
is no big deal. Only a month ago, I
contemplated suicide — failing finances,
failed love, the usual flighty things.
Since then, I've found a panacea,
treating friends and family to dinners.
At least I'm still of use. But given
the demise of print journalism,
who will investigate the sins?
Who will remind me of the world
beyond my variable gut, my silly
jowls, or the way a habitual meal
is not all there should be to life?

REGIME CHANGE

Thirteen-year-old Hamza's parents
have posted pictures of their
dead son on the internet
to prove the torture instituted
by the Syrian regime. His knees
are crushed, his body mutilated.
His father fainted when he first
saw the corpse of his son.

Some say it's time for action,
pretending to champion
democracy. Instead, another
chance to kill for peace —
the peace of broken knees,
peace that pumps life
out of the poor and money
into the pockets of the rich.

Hamza lies, shattered, on
a cotton blanket. Make yourself
look. War, torture? Pleasure
people feel when power
transcends reason. In the streets
people are chanting, "Kill
the child killers," but
the battle to win is within.

THE POLITICS OF PROMISES

If they were favorite china
dishes shattered on kitchen tiles,
we'd sweep the shards
with a bristle brush,
sigh for what can't be fixed
and whisper our gratitude
that nothing cut our foot.

A bone when broken,
for all the sudden shock
and searing pain, the possible
surgery and pins, will heal
with the consolation that
fractures mend stronger
where they were broken.

But the economy is ephemeral,
nothing a poor person can
grasp when just getting
to the job costs an hour's pay
and forty hours doesn't
cover basics — assuming
the boss lets you work full time.

We were promised the American
dream. As if. Then, there's
what we call "the party system."
A broken dish we know is gone.
The broken promises just go on.
What kind of party only allows
the rich and powerful to celebrate?

THE IMPENDING ELECTION

Here are your choices. Vote
for the candidate who steals openly or
secretly, who lies plainly or with a coy smile.
Vote for those who promise more or less
knowing there's no chance to deliver.
Vote — our American privilege,
franchise, duty. Vote, to promote the illusion
of freedom. Vote, to assuage your sorry
conscience which, otherwise, would
keep you sleepless. Get up from
that comfortable couch, go out
even in heavy rain, bravely
trek to the polling place ignoring
the clear omen of the storm,
the near-gale winds splattering
campaign fliers into gutters where
last-ditch volunteers beseech you to
vote. For a drink. Vote for a cigar.
Vote for a pretty haircut. Vote for the one
who kills in defense or the candidate who
kills to win. It's the American way.
Pick the lesser of two evils.
Or don't vote and pick no evil.

THE OTHER FACTS

Red has a frequency between
430 and 480 terahertz. This is
indisputable for me, though I see
red when someone won't listen.
It should be easy to convince
a person with facts. I could say,
"That's a lovely red sweater
you are wearing." You might
blush, and call it flattery
but you couldn't say, "I
disagree. It's blue." We
can express our tastes —
whether one color is
prettier than another.

But on physical facts we
must agree. Not so in our society.
Not so in the classroom, where
every student is a customer.
"The professor is preaching
red ideas and they offend me."
And the professor, there to
please, must relent or change
the facts to a different frequency.
Or in politics, a candidate

for president says, "I know it
isn't true but I can say it
anyway. In politics, that's
just what we do."

Ordinary folks think, "My
opinion is as good as yours,"
but not all opinions are factual
or true. And that, good sir
or madam, is why someone
is going to kill you, fully
convinced his cause is just
and you, misinformed
and miscreant, should perish.
Much as you try to reason
with him, you can't win.
Everything is just "your opinion."
For the people with the guns,
only their facts are true.

HAPPY MEALS

First out the drive-up window
comes a Coke with ice, glistening
with moisture, long straw sticking
from its slightly open lid. Then,
the box, bedecked with images
from the latest kiddie film.

Eat half the cookies, followed
by small fries, three of the four
chicken nuggets. Open the plastic
toy — an LED figure made in China.

One more squeeze of ketchup
on a lingering fry. Then, out
the car window it all goes, littered
along the roadside as the kids
complain, "I'm bored. There's
nothing to do at home."

WAY DOWN UPON

The sign reads, "Welcome
to the Historic Suwannee River"
where a State Park features
dioramas depicting happy slaves.
Is Stephen Foster even still allowed?
Amos 'N' Andy is long gone.
Who really misses Sambo or Uncle
Remus? And while Bill Cosby
didn't really buy *Our Gang*
to banish a sing-song, "eeny
meeny miny," gratefully we
don't catch anyone who rhymes
with "moe" the way we used to.

But colleges now recommend
we drop *Huck Finn* and *Heart
of Darkness,* lest we offend.
Textbooks must be PC. There is
token progress everywhere,
and yes, we need to be on guard.
We shouldn't just teach old,
dead white guys. Prejudice is so
enshrined, when they play "Dixie"
at Stone Mountain, some people still
shout, "The South will rise again."
But censorship, like stupidity is
the cause, not cure for prejudice.

IN THE AIRPORT

1. Rocking Chairs

Tall, white, with wood-slatted bottoms —
rockers facing the tarmac. A kid kicking
like he's pumping on a swing. A woman
with an aluminum walker, motionless
with a glassy grin. A mother nursing.
Comfort for the nervous traveler who
stayed awake all night in his motel.

2. The 15' x 24' Flag

For all its size, people barely
notice the 15' x 24' flag hanging
motionless from the ceiling
of the atrium. Beneath it, three
soldiers in desert camouflage
kill an hour before flying
home for two weeks of leave.
Then, it's two more years
of active duty and IEDs.
Three soldiers look up
longingly at their flag.

3. Saxophonist in an Airport

He's scored an airport gig
playing mellow jazz over
a computerized rhythm section.
His riffs are virtuous,

short of virtuoso, but
he's earning his tuition —
a music major aimed at
teaching high school.

He must admire Grover
Washington, gliding over
the backbeat, phrasing
a well-practiced "Simply
Beautiful." The airport
management thinks he's
a touch of class, but his
tip jar still has only
five dollars he put in
to cue folks and so far,
from eleven to one,
he's sold only one CD.

4. Waiting at the Gate

The three-year-old jumping jack
boy tugging toward the plane.

The hoodied teen with pants
at half-ass jiving to an iPod.

A pink sweat-suited twenty-
something female athlete.

A thirty-or-so male executive
judging from his black attaché.

The forty-plus woman reading

her romance novel with her lips.

The cashmered first-class woman
whose perfect makeup hides her fifties.

A late-sixties intellectual
writing his observations.

The seventy-ish Humpty Dumpty
man taking Tums.

The mid-eighties woman trembling
as she is wheeled aboard.

AT THE REST STOP

There's a state map
with a red pushpin
reassuring us, "You
are here."

The display case is
filled with posters:
"Have you seen ... ?"
"Missing since ... "

Fifteen children,
ages one to seventeen,
some gone for years.
Age-progression imaging

a baby who would be three,
a five-year-old, now ten.
"Missing since ... "
"Have you seen ... ?"

An attendant cleans
the glass, dusts the cases.
Motorists, relieved,
hurry on their way.

"Have you seen ... ?"
"Missing since ... "

TO BE SOMEWHERE

For Henny Youngman

"Everyone has to be somewhere,"
the man in the closet said. He was
hiding across from the bed when
her husband came home.

What else can we do, looking
for people who don't tear us down,
or better, offer a decent meal,
a soft bed, a little nooky?

Along the highway, signs mark
little towns where aging mechanics
keep aging cars in suspension. Houses
need paint but no law compels it.

Except for a stiff wind or some
nagging, fixing a broken window
is optional. What must we do,
nestled five or ten miles off the inter-
state, in a place hard to remember
or pronounce? It is, at least, somewhere.

THE CHILEAN WOMAN

The Chilean woman turns
the pages of *Forbes* like
a picture book, fixing her
eyes on gentlemen in blue
three-piece suits and women
with attachés. She wears
a scarf from the Andes
and dungarees. Names
are slowly called into
the mammography clinic.

Maybe she won't need surgery.

The doctor's name is
snipped from the address
tab on the magazine cover.
His Lexus is parked in
the free doctors' lot. Her
husband's old pickup is
angled at the edge of
the patients' parking.
$2.50 an hour. Medicaid
may not pay for her procedure.

THE DOCTOR WHO BROUGHT THE NEWS

He arrives as grim as a reaper,
hovering over his patient's bedside,
covers half his face with
the test-bearing clipboard
and prefaces his slow revelation
with, "I'm the one who has
to bring bad news." He
pauses to let that set in
as the man who had brain
surgery squeezes his pale
wife's hand. "But this time
I'm surprised to say the
tumor is benign." Who
told the doctor he had to
build suspense. They
ask him, "Please repeat that."

ICU WAITING ROOM

The eyes say, "I'm going
to cry," though the clenched
jaw says not to. Tears grow
in her eyes but not enough
to drop. She lets out a sigh
and that is all it takes.

He lingers in a corner,
seated on a sofa, his body
stiff in resolution. He reads
 a year-old copy of *Sports
Illustrated* noting how they
got the predictions wrong.

She is the one with religion,
but prayers aren't much
consolation. He is the rebel
who moved out early. "No
more church for me." Now,
their mother is eighty-three.

Her shoulders slump
in the big stuffed chair
and she relaxes into sobs.
Hearing her, he rises
to pat her heaving back,
and lies, "It's up to God."

I WANT TO LOVE YOUR WIFE

For women's studies pioneer, Merlin Stone, née Marilyn Jacobson, 1931-2011, author of When God Was a Woman.

I never met her but
I want to love her
at least a little, for you,
my new friend, were
her friend, her fan, her
worshipper, married to her
for thirty-four years
before illness first
weakened her, rendered
her mute, then stole her
from you. When I
search her name
four million links appear.
She was famous,
gorgeous, brilliant,
which you can prove
to me with clippings
in albums, books she
wrote, even her resonant
voice responding to
an interviewer on CD.
I have to love your wife
or we can't be friends.
Not that you've compelled
me. Not that you've

aimed some figurative gun,
but, in fact, her studies of
Goddesses are what I
might read for fun
and also, when I learn
to love your wife,
it will teach that
male-chauvinist bastard,
Death, that he can't win.

HOW SUDDENLY

You aren't senior to me enough
that I can call you old, but what
seized you? Suddenly you are
a wheezing skeleton, white hair
combed back to emphasize your
frailty. Someone whispers,
"cancer," and another, "stroke."
We've both been prodigal though
you were better at it — weed, whisky,
long, late nights. Nothing that really
warrants punishment. We've both
survived our arguments but how
can we stay friends if you
consort with mortality?

REAL MEN DON'T SMELL GARDENIAS

I know you are not a phony
because, in the midst of an
earnest to intense round of golf,
clattering along a path
between the fifth and sixth holes,
you stop the cart, pick two
white gardenias, breathe
deeply, and hand me one,
the aroma of which perfumes
the afternoon. From such
unabashed joy — from such lapses
in the order you otherwise impose —
a real friendship could be built.

THE PERSISTENCE OF FLOWERS

1.
The gardenia grows
scrawny, too-tall thin
branches, barely a leaf
left. Yet, its tight, white
bud has opened to offer
a perfume purer than
any Parisian luxury.

2.
The overgrowth of honey-
suckle vines, reaches
above the chain link fence,
obscuring the backyard
clutter, uncut lawn —
so sweet it makes up for
a neighbor's other sins.

3.
The profusion of small,
white trellis roses,
a hundred blossoms
woven over the front
walk, force us to duck
their thorns as they
welcome with their aroma.

4.
An eighty-year-old
Linden tree's blossoms,
dangling from vast arms
all of June, imbue the streets
and every passing stranger
with the pungency of summer.

THE LIVE OAK

The Old Moody Homestead Oak in Bunnell, Florida,
is estimated to be four hundred years old.

Those who have split wood
know not to wedge where
limbs branch. Nature builds
stronger than steel.
That juncture supports five
tons or more, has held
for hundreds of years.
Weather never mattered —
wait a decade, the drought
will ease. Even its ferns,
curled brown across its bark,
are classified, "Resurrection,"
opening green with just
a little rain. Resistant
to any natural force —
dozens of hurricanes —
avoiding the stupidity
of saws, the old oak
survives in silent solidity.

THE SNOWBIRD'S SONNET

The promise of an endless summer brought
me here. Daytona Beach, with hard, flat sand,
green surf, an amphitheater where a band
performs for free on summer nights. I thought
the warmth of Florida would compensate
for all the ice and snow I had to clear —
an end to winter doldrums and the fear
I'd never leave that endless, frozen state.
I hadn't calculated how far north
I picked, or how one summer thins the blood,
so nights in forties, days just sixty would
require a jacket when I venture forth.
It isn't freezing. Sure, I'm glad for that.
I wear a bathing suit and woolen hat.

IN COUNTY KILDARE

1. Old Man Fishing

The old man fishing for pike
in River Barrow, has walked
a mile out of town to where
the weeds along the bank are
cool and buggy enough for a fish
to take a holiday. He casts a fly
only ten feet out and draws it
slowly in at least two times
a minute. "They can be this big,"
he says with hands spread much
too wide to believe, but why
correct him? The conservation
sign nearby says, "All fish must
be returned live back to the river."

2. Desmond Egan at the Irish Music Concert

He's seated but
he's dancing a reel,
heel and toe under
his seat. The audience
surprised as he shouts,
"Lovely, lovely."
Smiling broadly,
as if just listening
were not enough,

he calls the fiddler's
name, "Malachy, Malachy."

Later I ask, "Why
did you keep calling out?"
"You wouldn't think it,"
he says, "but musicians
are the meekest souls.
They need our reassurance."

WHY YOU EAT FISH EYES

"My mother ate the fish eyes,"
you say. Not just the little white
meat in the cheeks which is sweet,
but the yellowed eyes, which
squirt a bitter gel. And you
eat them, too, but why?
Out of duty to mom —
who told you how she starved,
a war orphan forced to accept
any scrap of food and the affection
of the older man they made
her marry. Your mother,
for all her suffering, felt
justified to beat you.
Staring straight ahead, you
declare, "My mother loved these,"
biting, chewing thoroughly
before you swallow with
a determined grin.

THE MAGICIAN

You must be adept to do magic —
clean moves, perfect palms, pulls
that confound even colleagues.
Then, there are the prop makers,
so clever their wooden boxes
dissolve their contents. Careful
examination doesn't always
reveal how. Stage magic or
closeup, it isn't all just tricks.
It's the persona — the cynic,
the clown, the whiner and
the bold show-off. Clever
in my own way, I'll play
the perfect straightman
smiling as I'm sawed in half.

FOUR SHOTS

1. The Death of Them

She had a vagina
like a slaughterhouse.
He had a penis
like a sword.
Was it a suicide
pact or love?

2. Gallows Humor

The trick is knowing
when to step aside before
the trapdoor opens.

3. Love Shows

Man in Speedo suit.
Woman in a bikini.
See what he's thinking.

4. Double Books

He fears the IRS, living
a sub rosa life as if his extra
earnings were hard crimes.
She keeps a set of double books:
writing love poems
with no one to read them.

PEACE PRIZES

1. A Man and a Woman

I want to be a feminist
but anatomy is destiny.
I don't have breasts so
maybe that's why I
eye them — not so directly,
just glancing at women
as they pass. Each has
what men need more of —
the capacity to nurture.

2. Peace Anyway

World peace would be
a catastrophe: unemployed
soldiers, weapons makers
out of jobs, bases closed.
The banks would fail if
the military goes bust,
and trust me, world
population will explode.

And what of poets? Who
will want their odes to peace?
What will we protest? But, rest
easy, it's highly unlikely
the killing will cease, though
I'd chance it anyway.

TAPS

If you see my fingers tapping
it's a mantra not a disease.
I'm counting syllables — *om
mani bêmê hum* — the way some
count their Rosaries — a chant
for peace. Or, *om mani padme
hum* — a chant for health. Tapping
at odd moments, to stay calm,
to ward off pain, or find quiet
in a chaotic world. At night,
in bed, it only takes eight
repetitions before I fall asleep.

DECLARATION OF VICTORY

If you think this is a suicide note
then every door marked exit is
a tragedy. The push-bar required
on public doors is simpler even than
a doorknob. Hit it with a hand or
throw yourself against it in a panic.
The door bursts outward, and if
it's day, a sun may greet you
brighter than you've ever known.
If night, a blackness envelops you
closer than ever under the covers
where you hid as a kid. Warm
breath of death. Expiration
that is an inspiration. What is
sad about an end to pain? Eyes
that aged sooner from all the bullies
poking at them. Throat strangled
from my birth to this day. The stress
in my neck and shoulders.
The constant rotting in my guts.
All that sexual conflict. A body
not to be trusted and a mind that suffers
more than any organ. For those who
believe death is an ending — *fini*.
For those who want death to be more
— an opening to other realms — fine.
For those who wish hell on me,
I love my weather hotter, hotter.
Victory!

ABOUT THE AUTHOR

Dr. David B. Axelrod has published hundreds of articles and poems as well as twenty-one books of poetry. Among many grants and honors, he is the recipient of three Fulbright Awards, and he served as the first official Fulbright Poet-in-Residence in the People's Republic of China. On Long Island, he founded and directed Writers Unlimited Agency, Inc. and Writers Ink Press. There, he also served as Suffolk County Poet Laureate. He has shared the stage with such notables as Louis Simpson, X. J. Kennedy, William Stafford, Robert Bly, Allen Ginsberg, David Ignatow and Galway Kinnell. He represented the United States at the Struga Festival, performed at the U.N., and for the American Library Association. He has appeared at hundreds more schools and public events. His poetry has been translated and published in sixteen languages and he is a frequent and celebrated master teacher. He now resides with his wife, Sandy, in Daytona Beach, Florida, where he founded and directs the Creative Happiness Institute, Inc.

Websites:

http://www.poetrydoctor.org

and

http://www.creativehappiness.org

CPSIA information can be obtained at www.ICGtesting.com
Printed in the USA
LVOW01s0617270514

387385LV00002B/4/P